Acid Reflux Diet Cookbook

A Flavorful Journey with Acid Reflux-Friendly Recipes

Copyright-All Rights Reserved

This book has copyright protection. You can use the book for personal purpose. You should not see, use, alter, distribute, quote, take excerpts or paraphrase in part or whole the material contained in this book without obtaining the permission of the author first.

Table Of Contents

Introduction — 1

Food to Avoid In GERD — 3

Breakfast — 5

Lunch — 16

Dinner — 27

Desserts — 38

Snacks — 48

Seafood — 59

Introduction

Welcome to a gastronomic journey designed to bring relief and joy to those seeking a reprieve from the discomfort of acid reflux. In "The Acid Reflux Diet Cookbook," we embark on a flavorful exploration of a culinary landscape where delicious meets digestive ease.

For many, the battle against acid reflux can be a daily struggle, impacting not only what we eat but also our overall well-being. This cookbook aims to be a trusted companion on your journey to finding culinary solutions that not only satiate your taste buds but also promote digestive health.

Our approach is rooted in the belief that maintaining a diet for acid reflux doesn't mean sacrificing taste or variety. Within these pages, you'll discover a collection of thoughtfully crafted recipes that prioritize ingredients known for their digestive-friendly qualities. From nourishing soups to delightful mains and guilt-free desserts, each dish is designed to be both a treat for your palate and a balm for your digestive system.

Our philosophy is based on the idea that flavour and diversity don't have to be sacrificed in order to adhere to an acid reflux diet. You'll find a selection of carefully planned recipes in these pages that highlight foods that are well-known for being easy on the stomach. Each meal, which ranges from filling soups to delicious main courses and guilt-free sweets, is meant to satisfy your palette while also soothing your digestive tract.

We are aware that everyone has different tastes and sensitivity levels when it comes to their journey towards gastronomic wellbeing. To ensure that there is something for everyone, regardless of dietary restrictions or level of culinary skill, this cookbook includes a variety of recipes.

Food to Avoid In GERD

Gastroesophageal Reflux Disease (GERD) demands a conscientious approach to dietary choices, and understanding which foods to avoid is paramount in managing its symptoms. Certain items have been consistently identified as potential triggers for acid reflux, exacerbating discomfort and undermining the effectiveness of symptom management strategies.

Highly acidic foods, such as citrus fruits and tomatoes, stand out as prominent culprits. The acidity in these fruits can provoke the production of stomach acid, worsening GERD symptoms. Similarly, caffeinated beverages like coffee and tea, as well as carbonated drinks, can relax the lower esophageal sphincter (LES), allowing stomach acid to splash into the esophagus.

Fatty and fried foods are also notorious contributors to GERD symptoms. These items take longer to digest, leading to prolonged stomach distension and an increased likelihood of acid reflux. Chocolate, mint, and spicy foods, though delightful to the palate, can relax the LES and stimulate acid production, making them unwelcome additions to a GERD-friendly diet.

In the realm of beverages, alcohol is a known antagonist for GERD sufferers. It not only relaxes the LES but also directly irritates the esophagus lining, intensifying discomfort. Additionally, large meals and late-night snacking can exacerbate symptoms, as a full stomach puts increased pressure on the LES, promoting acid reflux.

Understanding these dietary triggers empowers individuals with GERD to make informed choices that align with their wellness goals. By conscientiously avoiding these problematic foods, individuals can complement medical interventions with lifestyle changes, fostering a more comprehensive and effective approach to managing GERD symptoms. In the subsequent sections, we will explore in greater detail the alternatives and substitutes that can transform your meals into soothing allies against the challenges posed by Gastroesophageal Reflux Disease.

Breakfast

Oatmeal with Banana Slices

Ingredients:
1/2 cup old-fashioned oats
1 cup almond milk (or any non-citrus, non-dairy milk)
1 ripe banana, sliced
1 tablespoon honey
1/2 teaspoon ground cinnamon (optional)
1 tablespoon chia seeds (optional, as they can be soothing for some individuals)

Instructions:
In a saucepan, combine the oats and almond milk.
Cook over medium heat, stirring frequently, until the oats have absorbed the liquid and reached your desired consistency.
Once the oats are cooked, stir in the sliced banana.
Add honey to the oatmeal and mix well. Adjust the amount to your desired sweetness.
If you like, sprinkle ground cinnamon over the oatmeal for added flavor. Cinnamon is generally well-tolerated by many individuals with acid reflux, but if you find it bothersome, you can skip it.
Add chia seeds for additional texture and potential soothing properties.
Allow the oatmeal to cool for a few minutes before eating.
Spoon the oatmeal into a bowl and enjoy your reflux-friendly breakfast.

Greek Yogurt Parfait

Ingredients:
1 cup plain, non-fat Greek yogurt: Greek yogurt is often better tolerated than regular yogurt for individuals with acid reflux.
1/2 cup granola: Choose a low-fat, low-sugar granola option. Look for one that doesn't contain acidic fruits or excessive spices.
1/2 cup ripe berries (e.g., strawberries, blueberries, or raspberries): Berries are generally well-tolerated by many individuals with acid reflux.
1 tablespoon honey or maple syrup: Use a small amount for sweetness.
1 tablespoon slivered almonds or chopped walnuts (optional)

Instructions:
Layer the Yogurt: Start with a layer of Greek yogurt at the bottom of a glass or bowl.
Add Berries: Add a layer of ripe berries on top of the yogurt.
Sprinkle Granola: Sprinkle a layer of granola over the berries. Make sure the granola is low in fat and sugar.
Drizzle Honey or Maple Syrup: Drizzle a small amount of honey or maple syrup over the granola for sweetness. Adjust the amount based on your preference.
Optional Nuts: If you tolerate nuts well, add a tablespoon of slivered almonds or chopped walnuts for extra texture.
Repeat Layers: Repeat the layering process until you reach the top of the glass or bowl, finishing with a drizzle of honey or maple syrup on the top.
Let it Set: Allow the parfait to set for a few minutes to let the flavors meld together.
Serve and Enjoy: Use a long spoon to get a bit of each layer in each bite.

Egg White Omelet

Ingredients:

3 large egg whites: Separate the egg whites from the yolks. You can save the yolks for other recipes or discard them.

1/4 cup diced bell peppers: Choose non-spicy vegetables like bell peppers, which are generally well-tolerated.

1/4 cup diced tomatoes: Tomatoes can be acidic, but in moderation, they might be okay for some individuals. If you're sensitive, you can omit them.

1/4 cup chopped spinach: Spinach is a low-acid, nutrient-rich leafy green.

1/4 cup diced mushrooms: Mushrooms can add flavor and texture without being too harsh on the stomach.

Salt and pepper to taste: Use sparingly, especially with salt, as excessive salt intake can contribute to reflux.

1 teaspoon olive oil or non-stick cooking spray: Use a minimal amount of oil for cooking.

Instructions:

Prepare Vegetables: Dice the bell peppers, tomatoes, and mushrooms.

Whisk Egg Whites: In a bowl, whisk the egg whites until they are well combined and slightly frothy.

Cook Vegetables: Heat a non-stick skillet over medium heat. Add 1 teaspoon of olive oil or use non-stick cooking spray. Saute the bell peppers, tomatoes, mushrooms, and spinach until they are softened.

Pour Egg Whites: Pour the whisked egg whites over the cooked vegetables in the skillet.

Season: Add salt and pepper to taste. Remember to go easy on the salt.

Cook the Omelet: Allow the egg whites to set at the edges. Gently lift the edges with a spatula, letting the uncooked egg flow underneath.

Fold and Serve: Once the egg whites are mostly set, fold the omelet in half using the spatula. Cook for another minute or until the omelet is fully cooked but still moist.

Serve Warm: Slide the omelet onto a plate and serve warm.

Whole Grain Toast with Almond Butter

Ingredients:
1-2 slices of whole grain bread: Choose a whole grain or whole wheat option for added fiber.
1-2 tablespoons almond butter: Opt for natural almond butter without added sugars or oils.
1 ripe banana, sliced: Bananas are usually well-tolerated and can add natural sweetness.
Optional: a drizzle of honey or a sprinkle of chia seeds: If you want extra sweetness, you can add a small amount of honey. Chia seeds can also provide additional texture and some individuals find them soothing.

Instructions:
Toast the Bread: Toast the whole grain bread slices to your desired level of crispiness.
Spread Almond Butter: Once the toast is ready, spread a generous layer of almond butter on each slice.
Add Banana Slices: Arrange the banana slices evenly on top of the almond butter.
Optional Toppings: If desired, drizzle a small amount of honey over the top or sprinkle chia seeds for added texture.
Serve and Enjoy: Place the slices on a plate and enjoy your reflux-friendly whole grain toast with almond butter.

Banana Walnut Muffins

Ingredients:
1 1/2 cups mashed ripe bananas (about 3-4 medium bananas)
1/2 cup unsweetened applesauce
1/4 cup melted coconut oil or a mild-flavored oil
1/2 cup honey or maple syrup
1 teaspoon vanilla extract
2 large eggs
1 3/4 cups whole wheat flour
1 teaspoon baking soda
1/2 teaspoon salt
1 teaspoon ground cinnamon
1/2 cup chopped walnuts

Instructions:
Preheat the Oven: Preheat your oven to 350°F (175°C). Line a muffin tin with paper liners.
Prepare Wet Ingredients: In a large bowl, combine the mashed bananas, applesauce, melted coconut oil, honey or maple syrup, vanilla extract, and eggs. Mix well.
Combine Dry Ingredients: In a separate bowl, whisk together the whole wheat flour, baking soda, salt, and ground cinnamon.
Mix Wet and Dry Ingredients: Gradually add the dry ingredients to the wet ingredients, stirring until just combined. Avoid overmixing.
Fold in Walnuts: Gently fold in the chopped walnuts into the batter.
Fill Muffin Cups: Spoon the batter into the prepared muffin cups, filling each about two-thirds full.
Bake: Bake in the preheated oven for 18-20 minutes or until a toothpick inserted into the center comes out clean.
Cool: Allow the muffins to cool in the tin for a few minutes before transferring them to a wire rack to cool completely.

Smoothie Bowl

Ingredients:
Smoothie Base:
1 cup plain, non-fat Greek yogurt
1/2 cup frozen berries (such as blueberries, strawberries, or raspberries)
1/2 ripe banana
1/2 cup almond milk (or any non-citrus, non-dairy milk)
1 tablespoon honey (optional, for sweetness)
1 tablespoon chia seeds (optional, for added texture and potential soothing properties)
Toppings:
Sliced banana
Sliced strawberries
Granola (choose a low-fat, low-sugar option)
Slivered almonds or chopped walnuts (optional)
Unsweetened coconut flakes
Fresh mint leaves for garnish

Instructions:
Prepare the Smoothie Base:
In a blender, combine the Greek yogurt, frozen berries, ripe banana, almond milk, honey (if using), and chia seeds (if using).
Blend until smooth and creamy.
Pour into a Bowl:
Pour the smoothie into a bowl, ensuring a smooth and even surface.
Add Toppings:
Arrange sliced banana, sliced strawberries, granola, slivered almonds or chopped walnuts (if using), and unsweetened coconut flakes on top of the smoothie base.
Garnish:
Garnish with fresh mint leaves for a burst of flavor.
Serve and Enjoy:
Use a spoon to scoop up a bit of each layer with each bite.
This smoothie bowl provides a balance of flavors and textures while incorporating ingredients that are generally well-tolerated by individuals with acid reflux. Adjust the recipe based on your personal preferences and sensitivities

Egg and Spinach Breakfast Wrap

Ingredients:
2 large eggs
1 cup fresh spinach, washed and chopped
1 whole-grain or low-acid tortilla
1/4 cup feta cheese, crumbled (optional)
1 tablespoon olive oil
Salt and pepper to taste

Instructions:

Cook Spinach:

Heat olive oil in a pan over medium heat. Add chopped spinach and sauté until wilted. Season with a pinch of salt and pepper. Set aside.

Scramble Eggs:

In the same pan, scramble the eggs. You can whisk them in a bowl before adding them to the pan. Season with salt and pepper to taste.

Assemble the Wrap:

Warm the tortilla in the pan or microwave for a few seconds.
Place the scrambled eggs down the center of the tortilla.
Add the sautéed spinach on top of the eggs.
Sprinkle crumbled feta cheese (if using) over the spinach.

Fold and Serve:

Fold the sides of the tortilla over the filling, creating a wrap.

Optional: Toast or Grill (Optional):

If you prefer a warm and toasty wrap, you can toast it on a grill or in a pan for a couple of minutes on each side.

Serve Warm:

Serve the egg and spinach breakfast wrap warm.

Feel free to customize this recipe based on your preferences and tolerances. If you have specific dietary concerns or restrictions, it's advisable to consult with a healthcare professional or a registered dietitian.

Pancakes with Blueberry Compote

Ingredients:
1 cup whole wheat flour
1 tablespoon sugar or honey
1 teaspoon baking powder
1/2 teaspoon baking soda
1/4 teaspoon salt
1 cup buttermilk (or a non-dairy alternative)
1 large egg
1 tablespoon melted unsalted butter (or a non-dairy alternative)
Cooking spray or a small amount of butter for the pan

Instructios:

Prepare the Dry Ingredients:
In a bowl, whisk together the whole wheat flour, sugar (or honey), baking powder, baking soda, and salt.

Combine Wet Ingredients:
In a separate bowl, whisk together the buttermilk, egg, and melted butter.

Mix Wet and Dry Ingredients:
Pour the wet ingredients into the dry ingredients and stir until just combined. It's okay if there are some lumps.

Cook Pancakes:
Heat a griddle or non-stick skillet over medium heat. Lightly coat the surface with cooking spray or a small amount of butter.

Pour 1/4 cup portions of batter onto the griddle for each pancake. Cook until bubbles form on the surface, then flip and cook the other side until golden brown.

Keep Warm:
Keep the cooked pancakes warm in a low oven while you make the blueberry compote.

Chia Seed and Berry Smoothie

Ingredients:
1 cup mixed berries (such as blueberries, strawberries, raspberries)
1 tablespoon chia seeds
1 cup plain, non-fat Greek yogurt
1/2 cup almond milk (or any non-citrus, non-dairy milk)
1 tablespoon honey (optional, for sweetness)
Ice cubes (optional)

Instructions:

Prepare the Berries:

If using fresh berries, wash them thoroughly. If using frozen berries, make sure they are unsweetened.

Combine Ingredients:

In a blender, combine the mixed berries, chia seeds, Greek yogurt, almond milk, and honey (if using).

Blend:

Blend until smooth. If the mixture is too thick, you can add more almond milk until you reach your desired consistency.

Adjust Sweetness:

Taste the smoothie and adjust sweetness by adding more honey if needed. Remember to go easy on sweeteners to keep it reflux-friendly.

Add Ice (Optional):

If you prefer a colder smoothie, you can add a handful of ice cubes and blend until smooth.

Serve:

Pour the smoothie into a glass and serve immediately.

Note: Chia seeds absorb liquid and can add thickness to the smoothie. If you let the smoothie sit for a while, it may thicken. If this happens and you prefer a thinner consistency, you can stir in more almond milk.

Turkey Sausage and Veggie Scramble

Ingredients:
1/2 lb lean ground turkey sausage
1 tablespoon olive oil
1/2 cup bell peppers, diced (choose non-spicy varieties)
1/2 cup zucchini, diced
1/2 cup cherry tomatoes, halved
4 large eggs
Salt and pepper to taste
Fresh herbs (such as parsley or chives) for garnish (optional)

Instructions:
In a large skillet, heat olive oil over medium heat. Add the ground turkey sausage and cook until browned, breaking it apart with a spoon as it cooks.
Add diced bell peppers, zucchini, and cherry tomatoes to the skillet. Cook until the vegetables are softened but still slightly crisp, about 3-5 minutes.
In a bowl, whisk the eggs until well combined. Pour the eggs over the turkey sausage and vegetables in the skillet.
Season with salt and pepper to taste. Remember to go easy on the salt, as excessive salt intake can contribute to reflux.
Gently scramble the eggs with the sausage and vegetables, stirring occasionally until the eggs are fully cooked.
Garnish with fresh herbs like parsley or chives for added flavor and freshness.
Serve the Turkey Sausage and Veggie Scramble warm.
This savory and protein-packed scramble is a reflux-friendly breakfast option. Feel free to customize the recipe with other non-acidic vegetables you enjoy. As always, if you have specific dietary concerns or restrictions, it's advisable to consult with a healthcare professional or a registered dietitian.

Lunch

Quinoa Salad with Cucumber and Mint

Ingredients:
For the Salad:
1 cup quinoa, rinsed and cooked according to package instructions
1 cucumber, diced
1/2 red onion, finely chopped
1/2 cup cherry tomatoes, halved
1/4 cup fresh mint leaves, chopped
1/4 cup feta cheese, crumbled (optional)

For the Dressing:
3 tablespoons olive oil
2 tablespoons fresh lemon juice
1 clove garlic, minced
Salt and pepper to taste

Instructions:
Rinse the quinoa under cold water. Cook it according to the package instructions. Once cooked, let it cool to room temperature.
Dice the cucumber, chop the red onion, halve the cherry tomatoes, and chop the fresh mint leaves.
In a large bowl, combine the cooked quinoa, diced cucumber, chopped red onion, cherry tomatoes, mint leaves, and crumbled feta cheese (if using).
In a small bowl, whisk together the olive oil, fresh lemon juice, minced garlic, salt, and pepper.
Pour the dressing over the quinoa salad and toss until all ingredients are well coated.
Refrigerate the salad for about 30 minutes before serving to allow the flavors to meld. This step is optional, and you can also serve it immediately.
Serve the Quinoa Salad with Cucumber and Mint as a refreshing and nutritious side dish. This salad is not only delicious but also rich in fiber and nutrients from the quinoa, vegetables, and fresh herbs. It's a great option for those with acid reflux. Adjust the recipe based on your preferences and sensitivities.

Mediterranean Chickpea Salad

Ingredients:
For the Salad:
2 cans (15 ounces each) chickpeas (garbanzo beans), drained and rinsed
1 cucumber, diced
1 cup cherry tomatoes, halved
1/2 red onion, finely chopped
1/2 cup Kalamata olives, pitted and sliced
1/2 cup crumbled feta cheese (optional)
1/4 cup fresh parsley, chopped

For the Dressing:
3 tablespoons extra-virgin olive oil
2 tablespoons red wine vinegar
1 clove garlic, minced
1 teaspoon dried oregano

Instructions:
Drain and rinse the chickpeas thoroughly.
In a large bowl, combine the chickpeas, diced cucumber, halved cherry tomatoes, chopped red onion, sliced Kalamata olives, crumbled feta cheese (if using), and chopped fresh parsley.
In a small bowl, whisk together the olive oil, red wine vinegar, minced garlic, dried oregano, salt, and pepper.
Pour the dressing over the chickpea salad and toss until all ingredients are well coated.
Refrigerate the salad for about 30 minutes before serving to enhance the flavors. This step is optional, and you can also serve it immediately.
Serve the Mediterranean Chickpea Salad as a refreshing and satisfying dish.
This salad is packed with fiber, protein, and a variety of nutrients, making it a nutritious and reflux-friendly option. Adjust the recipe based on your preferences and sensitivities.

Tuna Salad Lettuce Wraps

Ingredients:

For the Tuna Salad:
1 can (5 ounces) tuna, drained (choose tuna packed in water)
1/4 cup celery, finely chopped
2 tablespoons red onion, finely chopped
2 tablespoons mayonnaise (use a light or low-fat version if desired)
1 teaspoon Dijon mustard
Salt and pepper to taste
Fresh lemon juice (optional, for added flavor)

For the Lettuce Wraps:
Large lettuce leaves (such as butter or iceberg lettuce)
Avocado slices (optional, for added creaminess)
Cherry tomatoes, halved
Cucumber slices

Instructions:

In a bowl, combine the drained tuna, chopped celery, chopped red onion, mayonnaise, Dijon mustard, salt, and pepper. Mix well.

Add a squeeze of fresh lemon juice for added flavor, if desired.

Lay out large lettuce leaves on a flat surface.

Spoon a portion of the tuna salad onto each lettuce leaf.

Top the tuna salad with avocado slices, cherry tomato halves, and cucumber slices.

Fold the sides of the lettuce over the tuna salad and toppings to create a wrap.

Serve the Tuna Salad Lettuce Wraps chilled.

This recipe provides a low-carb alternative to traditional tuna salad sandwiches and is rich in protein and healthy fats

Vegetable and Lentil Soup

Ingredients:
1 cup dried green or brown lentils, rinsed and drained
1 tablespoon olive oil
1 onion, diced
2 carrots, peeled and diced
2 celery stalks, diced
3 cloves garlic, minced
1 teaspoon ground cumin
1 teaspoon ground coriander
1 teaspoon dried thyme
1 bay leaf
6 cups vegetable broth
1 can (14 ounces) diced tomatoes (choose low-acid variety)
2 cups chopped kale or spinach
Salt and pepper to taste
Fresh lemon juice (optional, for serving)

Instructions:
Rinse lentils under cold water and set them aside.
In a large pot, heat olive oil over medium heat. Add diced onion, carrots, and celery. Sauté until the vegetables are softened, about 5 minutes.
Add minced garlic, ground cumin, ground coriander, dried thyme, and bay leaf. Sauté for an additional 1-2 minutes until the spices are fragrant.
Add rinsed lentils, vegetable broth, and diced tomatoes (with their juice) to the pot. Bring the mixture to a boil.
Reduce heat to low, cover the pot, and let it simmer for about 25-30 minutes or until lentils are tender.
Stir in chopped kale or spinach and cook until wilted.
Season the soup with salt and pepper to taste. Adjust the seasoning as needed.Remove the bay leaf and ladle the soup into bowls. Optionally, squeeze fresh lemon juice over the soup just before serving for added brightness.
This Vegetable and Lentil Soup is not only delicious but also rich in fiber, protein, and various nutrients.

Avocado and Shrimp Salad

Ingredients:
For the Salad:
1 lb large shrimp, peeled and deveined
2 avocados, diced
1 cup cherry tomatoes, halved
1 cucumber, diced
1/4 cup red onion, finely chopped
1/4 cup fresh cilantro or parsley, chopped
Mixed salad greens (e.g., arugula, spinach, or lettuce)

For the Dressing:
3 tablespoons olive oil
2 tablespoons fresh lime juice
1 clove garlic, minced
Salt and pepper to taste

Instructions:
In a pot of boiling water, cook the shrimp for 2-3 minutes or until they turn pink and opaque. Drain and let them cool.
In a small bowl, whisk together olive oil, fresh lime juice, minced garlic, salt, and pepper to make the dressing.
In a large salad bowl, combine diced avocados, halved cherry tomatoes, diced cucumber, chopped red onion, and fresh cilantro or parsley.Add the cooked and cooled shrimp to the salad.
Drizzle the dressing over the salad and toss gently to coat everything evenly
Arrange a bed of mixed salad greens on individual plates. Spoon the avocado and shrimp mixture over the greens.
Garnish with additional cilantro or parsley if desired.
Serve the Avocado and Shrimp Salad immediately.
This salad is a great combination of creamy avocado, succulent shrimp, and fresh vegetables.

Grilled Chicken Salad

Ingredients:
For the Grilled Chicken:
2 boneless, skinless chicken breasts
2 tablespoons olive oil
1 teaspoon garlic powder
1 teaspoon paprika
Salt and pepper to taste
Lemon wedges for serving
For the Salad:
Mixed salad greens (e.g., romaine, spinach, arugula)
Cherry tomatoes, halved
Cucumber, sliced
Red onion, thinly sliced
Bell peppers, sliced (assorted colors)
Avocado, sliced
Feta cheese, crumbled (optional)

For the Dressing:
3 tablespoons extra-virgin olive oil
2 tablespoons balsamic vinegar
1 teaspoon Dijon mustard
1 clove garlic, minced
Salt and pepper to taste

Instructions:
In a bowl, mix olive oil, garlic powder, paprika, salt, and pepper. Coat the chicken breasts with the mixture.
Preheat the grill or grill pan over medium-high heat. Grill the chicken for about 6-8 minutes per side or until fully cooked.
Let the chicken rest for a few minutes before slicing. Squeeze fresh lemon juice over the grilled chicken slices.
In a large salad bowl, combine the mixed salad greens, cherry tomatoes, cucumber, red onion, bell peppers, avocado, and feta cheese (if using).
In a small bowl, whisk together olive oil, balsamic vinegar, Dijon mustard, minced garlic, salt, and pepper.
Place the grilled chicken slices on top of the salad.
Drizzle the dressing over the salad and chicken.
Toss the salad gently to coat everything with the dressing.
Divide the salad among individual plates and serve immediately.
Feel free to customize the salad by adding other ingredients like nuts, seeds, or your favorite vegetables.

Quinoa and Vegetable Bowl

Ingredients:
For the Quinoa:
1 cup quinoa, rinsed
2 cups water or vegetable broth
1/2 teaspoon salt
For the Vegetables:
2 tablespoons olive oil
1 bell pepper, diced (choose your preferred color)
1 zucchini, diced
1 cup cherry tomatoes, halved
1 cup broccoli florets
2 cloves garlic, minced

For the Dressing:
3 tablespoons extra-virgin olive oil
2 tablespoons balsamic vinegar
1 teaspoon Dijon mustard
1 clove garlic, minced
Salt and pepper to taste

Instructions:
In a medium saucepan, combine quinoa, water or vegetable broth, and salt. Bring to a boil, then reduce the heat to low, cover, and simmer for about 15 minutes or until the quinoa is cooked and water is absorbed. Remove from heat and let it sit, covered, for 5 minutes. Fluff with a fork.
In a large skillet, heat olive oil over medium heat. Add diced bell pepper, zucchini, cherry tomatoes, broccoli, and minced garlic. Sauté until the vegetables are tender but still crisp, about 5-7 minutes. Season with salt and pepper.
In a small bowl, whisk together olive oil, balsamic vinegar, Dijon mustard, minced garlic, salt, and pepper.
Divide the cooked quinoa among bowls. Top with sautéed vegetables.
Drizzle the dressing over the quinoa and vegetables.
Garnish with avocado slices, feta or goat cheese crumbles, and fresh herbs if desired.
Serve the Quinoa and Vegetable Bowl immediately.

Turkey and Avocado Wrap

Ingredients:
For the Wrap:
1 whole-grain or low-acid tortilla
4-6 slices of lean turkey breast
1/2 avocado, sliced
1/4 cup cucumber, thinly sliced
1/4 cup shredded lettuce or spinach
1 tablespoon mayonnaise (use a light or low-fat version if desired)

Optional Additions:
Tomato slices
Red onion, thinly sliced
Sprouts
Dijon mustard for extra flavor
Salt and pepper to taste

Instructions:

Slice the turkey, avocado, cucumber, and any additional ingredients you'd like to include.
If desired, warm the tortilla slightly in a dry skillet or microwave for a few seconds to make it more pliable.
Lay the tortilla flat and place the turkey slices in the center.
Layer the sliced avocado, cucumber, shredded lettuce or spinach, and any additional vegetables you choose.
Spread mayonnaise over the ingredients. You can also add Dijon mustard for extra flavor.
Season with a pinch of salt and pepper to taste.
Fold the sides of the tortilla over the filling, then roll it tightly from the bottom to create the wrap.
Optionally, slice the wrap in half diagonally and serve.
This Turkey and Avocado Wrap is a balanced and satisfying meal that's less likely to trigger acid reflux.

Salmon and Asparagus

Ingredients:
2 salmon fillets (about 6 ounces each), skin-on or skinless
1 bunch of asparagus, trimmed
2 tablespoons olive oil
2 cloves garlic, minced
1 teaspoon lemon zest
1 tablespoon lemon juice
Salt and pepper to taste
Fresh dill or parsley for garnish (optional)

Instructions:
Preheat the Oven:
Preheat your oven to 400°F (200°C).
Place the salmon fillets on one side of a baking sheet lined with parchment paper. Arrange the trimmed asparagus on the other side.
In a small bowl, whisk together olive oil, minced garlic, lemon zest, lemon juice, salt, and pepper
Brush the salmon fillets and asparagus with the marinade. Make sure to coat them evenly.
Bake in the preheated oven for about 12-15 minutes, or until the salmon is cooked through and flakes easily with a fork.
If you prefer a slightly crispy top on the salmon, you can broil it for an additional 1-2 minutes, watching carefully to prevent burning.
Sprinkle fresh dill or parsley over the salmon and asparagus for added freshness (optional).
Serve the salmon and asparagus hot, either as is or with a side of your choice (such as quinoa, rice, or a green salad).
This Salmon and Asparagus recipe is not only flavorful but also rich in omega-3 fatty acids, protein, and essential nutrients.

Brown Rice Stir-Fry

Ingredients:
For the Stir-Fry:
1 cup brown rice (cooked according to package instructions)
2 tablespoons olive oil or sesame oil
1 pound boneless, skinless chicken breasts or tofu, cut into bite-sized pieces
1 cup broccoli florets
1 bell pepper, thinly sliced
1 carrot, julienned
1 zucchini, sliced
2 cloves garlic, minced
1 tablespoon ginger, minced
Low-sodium soy sauce or tamari to taste
Salt and pepper to taste

Optional Toppings:
Green onions, chopped
Sesame seeds
Crushed red pepper flakes (if tolerated)

Instructions

Cook the brown rice according to the package instructions. Set aside.

If using chicken, season the chicken with salt and pepper. In a large wok or skillet, heat 1 tablespoon of oil over medium-high heat. Add the chicken and cook until fully cooked and browned on all sides. If using tofu, you can sauté it until golden in 1 tablespoon of oil or bake it separately.

In the same wok or skillet, add the remaining oil. Add garlic and ginger and sauté for about 30 seconds until fragrant. Add broccoli, bell pepper, carrot, and zucchini. Stir-fry for 3-5 minutes until the vegetables are tender-crisp.

Add the cooked brown rice to the wok or skillet, along with the cooked chicken or tofu. Drizzle low-sodium soy sauce or tamari over the stir-fry to taste. Toss everything together until well combined. Adjust salt and pepper if needed.

Garnish with chopped green onions, sesame seeds, and, if desired, crushed red pepper flakes for a bit of heat.

Serve the Brown Rice Stir-Fry hot.

This recipe provides a balance of whole grains, lean protein, and vegetables, making it a reflux-friendly option. Adjust the recipe based on your preferences and sensitivities.

Baked Chicken Breast with Herbs

Ingredients:
4 boneless, skinless chicken breasts
2 tablespoons olive oil
2 teaspoons dried thyme
2 teaspoons dried rosemary
1 teaspoon dried oregano
1 teaspoon garlic powder
1 teaspoon onion powder
Salt and pepper to taste
Lemon wedges for serving (optional)

Instructions:
Preheat your oven to 400°F (200°C).
Pat the chicken breasts dry with paper towels. This helps the herbs and spices adhere better.
Place the chicken breasts on a baking sheet lined with parchment paper.
In a small bowl, mix together olive oil, dried thyme, dried rosemary, dried oregano, garlic powder, onion powder, salt, and pepper.
Brush the herb and oil mixture over both sides of each chicken breast, ensuring they are well-coated.
Bake in the preheated oven for about 20-25 minutes or until the internal temperature reaches 165°F (74°C) and the chicken is cooked through.
If you prefer a slightly crispy top, you can switch to the broil setting for the last 2-3 minutes, watching carefully to prevent burning.
Allow the chicken to rest for a few minutes before serving. Squeeze fresh lemon juice over the chicken if desired.
Serve the Baked Chicken Breast with Herbs warm.
This recipe is low in fat and can be a good source of lean protein. The herbs add flavor without being overly spicy or acidic, making it a reflux-friendly option. Adjust the recipe based on your preferences and sensitivities

Grilled Vegetable and Quinoa Stuffed Peppers

Ingredients:
For the Stuffed Peppers:
4 large bell peppers, halved and seeds removed
1 cup quinoa, rinsed
2 cups vegetable broth or water
1 tablespoon olive oil
1 zucchini, diced
1 yellow squash, diced
1 red onion, diced
1 bell pepper (any color), diced
2 cloves garlic, minced
1 teaspoon dried oregano
1 teaspoon dried basil
Salt and pepper to taste

For the Grilling Marinade:
2 tablespoons balsamic vinegar
2 tablespoons olive oil
1 teaspoon Dijon mustard
1 teaspoon honey (optional)
Salt and pepper to taste

Instructions:
In a medium saucepan, combine quinoa and vegetable broth (or water). Bring to a boil, then reduce heat to low, cover, and simmer for about 15 minutes or until the quinoa is cooked and liquid is absorbed. Fluff with a fork.
Preheat your grill to medium-high heat.
In a small bowl, whisk together balsamic vinegar, olive oil, Dijon mustard, honey (if using), salt, and pepper to create the marinade.
In a large bowl, toss diced zucchini, yellow squash, red onion, and bell pepper with the marinade. Grill the vegetables until they are tender and have grill marks, about 8-10 minutes.
Sauté Quinoa and Garlic of olive oil. Add minced garlic and sauté for about 30 seconds. Add cooked quinoa, dried oregano, dried basil, salt, and pepper. Stir to combine.
Mix the grilled vegetables with the quinoa mixture. Adjust seasoning if needed.
Prepare Stuffed Peppersll pepper with the quinoa and grilled vegetable mixture.
Place the stuffed peppers on the preheated grill. Grill for about 10-15 minutes or until the peppers are tender and slightly charred.
Before serving, sprinkle crumbled feta or goat cheese and fresh parsley on top if desired.
Serve the Grilled Vegetable and Quinoa Stuffed Peppers warm.
These stuffed peppers are not only flavorful but also a great source of vegetables, fiber, and protein.

Salmon and Quinoa Bowl:

Ingredients:

For the Salmon:
2 salmon fillets
1 tablespoon olive oil
1 teaspoon lemon zest
1 tablespoon lemon juice
1 teaspoon dried dill
Salt and pepper to taste

For the Quinoa:
1 cup quinoa, rinsed
2 cups vegetable broth or water
1/4 cup chopped fresh parsley
1 tablespoon olive oil
Salt and pepper to taste

For the Dressing:
3 tablespoons extra-virgin olive oil
2 tablespoons balsamic vinegar
1 teaspoon Dijon mustard
1 clove garlic, minced
Salt and pepper to taste

For the Bowl:
2 cups mixed salad greens (e.g., spinach, arugula, or lettuce)
1 cucumber, sliced
1 cup cherry tomatoes, halved
1/4 cup red onion, thinly sliced
1/4 cup feta cheese, crumbled (optional)
Lemon wedges for serving

Instructions:

Preheat your oven to 400°F (200°C).

Place the salmon fillets on a baking sheet lined with parchment paper. In a small bowl, mix olive oil, lemon zest, lemon juice, dried dill, salt, and pepper. Brush the mixture over the salmon fillets.

Bake the salmon in the preheated oven for about 12-15 minutes or until the salmon is cooked through and flakes easily with a fork.

In a saucepan, combine quinoa and vegetable broth (or water). Bring to a boil, then reduce heat to low, cover, and simmer for about 15 minutes or until the quinoa is cooked and liquid is absorbed. Fluff with a fork. Stir in chopped parsley, olive oil, salt, and pepper.

In a small bowl, whisk together extra-virgin olive oil, balsamic vinegar, Dijon mustard, minced garlic, salt, and pepper.

In each serving bowl, assemble a bed of mixed salad greens. Add sliced cucumber, halved cherry tomatoes, and thinly sliced red onion.

Spoon the cooked quinoa over the vegetables. Top with the baked salmon fillets.

Drizzle the dressing over the bowl.

If desired, sprinkle crumbled feta cheese on top.

Serve the Salmon and Quinoa Bowl with lemon wedges on the side.

This bowl is not only delicious but also rich in omega-3 fatty acids, lean protein, and a variety of nutrients.

Vegetarian Stir-Fried Brown Rice

Ingredients:
2 cups cooked brown rice (preferably chilled)
2 tablespoons sesame oil or vegetable oil
1 onion, finely chopped
2 carrots, diced
1 bell pepper (any color), diced
1 cup broccoli florets
1 cup snap peas, ends trimmed
2 cloves garlic, minced
1 tablespoon soy sauce (low-sodium)
1 tablespoon hoisin sauce
1 teaspoon ginger, grated
2 green onions, chopped (for garnish)

Instructions:
Ensure that all vegetables are washed, chopped, and ready before starting.
Heat sesame oil or vegetable oil in a large wok or non-stick skillet over medium-high heat.
Add chopped onion and sauté for 2-3 minutes until it becomes translucent.
Add minced garlic and grated ginger. Sauté for an additional 30 seconds until fragrant.
Add diced carrots, bell pepper, broccoli florets, and snap peas. Stir-fry for 5-7 minutes or until the vegetables are tender-crisp.
Add the chilled cooked brown rice to the wok. Break up any clumps and stir-fry to combine with the vegetables.
Drizzle soy sauce and hoisin sauce over the rice and vegetables. Toss everything together until well-coated.
Taste and adjust the seasoning if needed. You can add more soy sauce or hoisin sauce according to your preference.
Garnish the stir-fried brown rice with chopped green onions and sesame seeds.
Serve the Vegetarian Stir-Fried Brown Rice hot. It can be enjoyed as a standalone dish or as a side.
Feel free to customize the vegetables and sauces based on your preferences. This recipe provides a healthy and flavorful vegetarian option with the nutritional benefits of brown rice and a variety of colorful vegetables. Adjust the recipe based on your sensitivities and dietary needs.

Turkey and Sweet Potato Skillet

Ingredients:
1 pound ground turkey
2 tablespoons olive oil
1 onion, finely chopped
2 cloves garlic, minced
2 medium-sized sweet potatoes, peeled and diced
1 bell pepper (any color), diced
1 teaspoon ground cumin
1 teaspoon paprika
1/2 teaspoon dried thyme
Salt and pepper to taste
1 cup low-sodium chicken broth
2 cups fresh spinach or kale, chopped

Instructions:
In a large skillet, heat olive oil over medium-high heat. Add ground turkey and cook until browned, breaking it apart with a spatula as it cooks.
Add chopped onion and minced garlic to the skillet. Sauté until the onion is softened and translucent.
Stir in diced sweet potatoes and bell pepper. Cook for about 5 minutes, allowing the vegetables to soften slightly.
Add ground cumin, paprika, dried thyme, salt, and pepper. Mix well to evenly coat the ingredients with the spices.
Pour the chicken broth into the skillet. Bring to a simmer and let it cook for about 10-15 minutes or until the sweet potatoes are tender.
Add chopped spinach or kale to the skillet. Stir until the greens are wilted.
Taste and adjust the seasoning if needed. Add more salt and pepper according to your preference.
Garnish the Turkey and Sweet Potato Skillet with fresh parsley if desired. Serve hot.
This recipe provides a balanced combination of lean protein from turkey, complex carbohydrates from sweet potatoes, and a variety of vegetables.

Baked Cod with Lemon

Ingredients:
4 cod fillets (about 6 ounces each)
2 tablespoons olive oil
2 tablespoons fresh lemon juice
2 cloves garlic, minced
1 teaspoon dried oregano
Salt and pepper to taste
Lemon slices for garnish
Fresh parsley, chopped, for garnish

Instructions:
Preheat your oven to 400°F (200°C).
Pat the cod fillets dry with paper towels and place them in a baking dish.
In a small bowl, whisk together olive oil, fresh lemon juice, minced garlic, dried oregano, salt, and pepper.
Pour the lemon marinade over the cod fillets, ensuring they are well-coated on both sides
For extra flavor, you can let the cod marinate in the refrigerator for about 15-30 minutes.
Bake the cod in the preheated oven for approximately 15-20 minutes or until the fish is opaque and flakes easily with a fork.
Garnish the baked cod with lemon slices and chopped fresh parsley.
Serve the Baked Cod with Lemon hot. You can pair it with your favorite side dishes such as steamed vegetables, quinoa, or a fresh green salad.
This recipe is simple, light, and allows the natural flavors of the cod to shine with the brightness of lemon.

Zucchini Noodles with Pesto

Ingredients:
For the Zucchini Noodles:
4 medium-sized zucchini, spiralized into noodles
1 tablespoon olive oil
Salt and pepper to taste

For the Pesto:
2 cups fresh basil leaves, packed
1/2 cup grated Parmesan cheese
1/3 cup pine nuts or walnuts
2 cloves garlic, peeled
1/2 cup extra-virgin olive oil
Salt and pepper to taste
Squeeze of fresh lemon juice (optional)

Optional Toppings:
Cherry tomatoes, halved
Grated Parmesan cheese
Red pepper flakes

Instructions:
1. Prepare Zucchini Noodles:
Use a spiralizer to turn the zucchini into noodles. If you don't have a spiralizer, you can use a julienne peeler or a knife to create thin strips. Place the zucchini noodles in a colander, sprinkle with salt, and let them sit for about 10 minutes to release excess moisture. Pat them dry with a paper towel.
In a food processor, combine fresh basil, grated Parmesan cheese, pine nuts or walnuts, and peeled garlic cloves. Pulse until the ingredients are finely chopped.
With the food processor running, slowly drizzle in the olive oil until the pesto reaches your desired consistency. Season with salt and pepper. If the pesto is too thick, you can add a bit more olive oil.
Taste the pesto and adjust the seasoning. Add a squeeze of fresh lemon juice if desired for extra brightness.
In a large skillet, heat 1 tablespoon of olive oil over medium heat. Add the zucchini noodles and toss for 2-3 minutes until just tender. Be careful not to overcook; you want them to retain a slight crunch.
Add the prepared pesto to the zucchini noodles and toss until well coated.
Garnish the Zucchini Noodles with Pesto with cherry tomatoes, additional grated Parmesan cheese, and red pepper flakes if desired.
Serve the Zucchini Noodles with Pesto immediately, either as a light main dish or as a side.

Chicken and Vegetable Skewers

Ingredients:
For the Marinade:
1.5 pounds boneless, skinless chicken breasts, cut into bite-sized pieces
1/4 cup olive oil
2 tablespoons soy sauce (low-sodium)
2 tablespoons honey
2 cloves garlic, minced
1 teaspoon dried oregano
1 teaspoon paprika
Salt and pepper to taste

For Garnish (optional):

Fresh parsley, chopped
Lemon wedges

For the Skewers:
Cherry tomatoes
Bell peppers (any color), cut into chunks
Red onion, cut into chunks
Zucchini, sliced

Instructions:
In a bowl, whisk together olive oil, soy sauce, honey, minced garlic, dried oregano, paprika, salt, and pepper to create the marinade.
Place the chicken pieces in a resealable plastic bag or a shallow dish. Pour half of the marinade over the chicken. Seal the bag or cover the dish and let it marinate in the refrigerator for at least 30 minutes (longer for more flavor). Reserve the remaining marinade for basting.
Preheat your grill or oven to medium-high heat.
Thread marinated chicken pieces, cherry tomatoes, bell pepper chunks, red onion chunks, and zucchini slices onto skewers, alternating the ingredients.
If grilling, place the skewers on the preheated grill. Grill for about 10-15 minutes, turning occasionally and basting with the reserved marinade until the chicken is cooked through and the vegetables are slightly charred.
If baking in the oven, place the skewers on a baking sheet lined with parchment paper. Bake in the preheated oven at 400°F (200°C) for about 20-25 minutes or until the chicken is cooked through.
Garnish the Chicken and Vegetable Skewers with chopped fresh parsley and serve with lemon wedges. Serve the skewers hot as a main dish, and pair them with your favorite side dishes like rice or a fresh salad.

Sweet Potato and Chickpea Curry

Ingredients:
- 2 medium-sized sweet potatoes, peeled and diced
- 1 can (15 oz) chickpeas, drained and rinsed
- 1 can (14 oz) diced tomatoes (preferably low-acid)
- 1 onion, finely chopped
- 2 cloves garlic, minced
- 1-inch piece of ginger, grated
- 1 can (13.5 oz) coconut milk (full-fat or light, based on preference)
- 1 tablespoon curry powder
- 1 teaspoon ground cumin
- 1 teaspoon ground coriander
- 1/2 teaspoon turmeric
- 1/2 teaspoon paprika
- Salt and pepper to taste
- 2 tablespoons olive oil
- Fresh cilantro, chopped (for garnish)
- Cooked rice or quinoa (for serving)

Instructions:

Heat the olive oil in a large pot over medium heat. Add the chopped onion and cook until softened.

Add the minced garlic and grated ginger, and sauté for an additional 1-2 minutes until fragrant.

Stir in the curry powder, cumin, coriander, turmeric, and paprika. Cook for another 1-2 minutes to toast the spices.

Add the diced sweet potatoes, chickpeas, and diced tomatoes to the pot. Stir well to combine.

Pour in the coconut milk and season with salt and pepper to taste. Bring the mixture to a simmer.

Reduce the heat to low, cover the pot, and let it simmer for about 20-25 minutes or until the sweet potatoes are tender.

Taste and adjust the seasoning if necessary. If you prefer a spicier curry, you can add a pinch of cayenne pepper.

Serve the curry over cooked rice or quinoa, and garnish with chopped fresh cilantro.

This curry is rich in flavor and should be relatively gentle on acid reflux

Baked Turkey Meatballs

Ingredients:
1 pound ground turkey (lean)
1/2 cup breadcrumbs (preferably whole wheat)
1/4 cup grated Parmesan cheese
1/4 cup milk (dairy or a non-dairy alternative)
1/4 cup finely chopped fresh parsley
1 teaspoon dried oregano
1 teaspoon dried basil
1/2 teaspoon garlic powder
1/2 teaspoon onion powder
Salt and pepper to taste
Olive oil (for greasing the baking sheet)

Instructions:
Preheat the oven to 400°F (200°C). Grease a baking sheet with a small amount of olive oil or line it with parchment paper.
In a large mixing bowl, combine the ground turkey, breadcrumbs, grated Parmesan cheese, milk, chopped parsley, dried oregano, dried basil, garlic powder, onion powder, salt, and pepper
Gently mix the ingredients until well combined, being careful not to overwork the meat.
Form the mixture into meatballs, about 1 to 1.5 inches in diameter, and place them on the prepared baking sheet.
Bake in the preheated oven for 20-25 minutes or until the meatballs are cooked through and golden brown on the outside. You can cut one open to ensure it's fully cooked.
Remove the meatballs from the oven and let them rest for a few minutes before serving.
Serve the turkey meatballs with a side of non-acidic tomato sauce or a creamy yogurt-based sauce.
Feel free to adjust the seasonings and spices according to your taste preferences. Additionally, pairing these meatballs with a non-acidic side, such as steamed vegetables or rice, can contribute to a reflux-friendly meal

Desserts

Baked Apples with Cinnamon

Ingredients:
4 medium-sized apples (such as Honeycrisp or Gala)
2 tablespoons melted unsalted butter or coconut oil
2 tablespoons honey or maple syrup (adjust to taste)
1 teaspoon ground cinnamon
1/4 teaspoon nutmeg (optional)
1/4 cup chopped nuts (such as almonds or walnuts) - optional for topping
Greek yogurt or a non-dairy alternative (optional for serving)

Instructions:
Preheat the oven to 375°F (190°C).
Wash and core the apples. If you have an apple corer, use it to remove the cores; otherwise, you can use a knife or spoon to carefully scoop out the seeds.
Place the cored apples in a baking dish.
In a small bowl, mix together the melted butter or coconut oil, honey or maple syrup, cinnamon, and nutmeg (if using).
Spoon the mixture over the apples, ensuring they are well-coated.
Bake in the preheated oven for 25-30 minutes or until the apples are tender. Cooking time may vary depending on the size and type of apples.
Optional: In the last 10 minutes of baking, sprinkle chopped nuts over the apples for added crunch.
Remove the baked apples from the oven and let them cool slightly before serving.
Serve the baked apples warm, optionally topped with a dollop of Greek yogurt or a non-dairy alternative.
This dessert is sweetened with natural sugars from the apples and a touch of honey or maple syrup, which can be more gentle on acid reflux. The cinnamon adds a warm and comforting flavor.

Banana Ice Cream

Ingredients:
4 ripe bananas, peeled, sliced, and frozen
1 teaspoon vanilla extract (optional)
Toppings of your choice (e.g., chopped nuts, shredded coconut, dark chocolate chips)

Instructions:
Slice the ripe bananas into small pieces.
Place the banana slices in a single layer on a parchment paper-lined tray or plate.
Freeze the banana slices for at least 2-3 hours or until solid.
Transfer the frozen banana slices to a high-powered blender or food processor.
Add the vanilla extract if desired.
Blend until the bananas are smooth and creamy. You may need to stop and scrape down the sides of the blender or food processor a few times.
Once the mixture reaches a creamy consistency, it's ready to be served.
You can serve it immediately for a soft-serve consistency, or transfer it to a container and freeze for a firmer texture.
Sprinkle your favorite toppings over the banana ice cream, such as chopped nuts, shredded coconut, or dark chocolate chips.
Scoop the banana ice cream into bowls or cones and enjoy your healthy and creamy treat!
Feel free to get creative with additional flavorings or mix-ins, such as a pinch of cinnamon or a tablespoon of nut butter. This banana ice cream is a great way to satisfy your sweet tooth with natural sugars from the bananas. It's also suitable for those with lactose intolerance or those looking for a dairy-free alternative to traditional ice cream.

Chia Seed Pudding

Ingredients:
1/4 cup chia seeds
1 cup unsweetened almond milk (or any milk of your choice)
1-2 tablespoons maple syrup or honey (adjust to taste)
1 teaspoon vanilla extract

Optional Toppings:
Fresh berries (strawberries, blueberries, raspberries)
Sliced bananas
Chopped nuts (almonds, walnuts)
Shredded coconut
Granola

Instructions:
In a bowl or jar, combine the chia seeds, almond milk, maple syrup or honey, and vanilla extract. Stir well to ensure that the chia seeds are evenly distributed.
Cover the bowl or jar and refrigerate the mixture for at least 3-4 hours or overnight. During this time, the chia seeds will absorb the liquid and create a pudding-like consistency.

After the first hour, stir the mixture again to prevent the chia seeds from clumping together. This step is optional but can help achieve a smoother texture.
Once the chia seed pudding has reached a thick and pudding-like consistency, it's ready to be served.
Customize your chia seed pudding by adding your favorite toppings. Fresh berries, sliced bananas, chopped nuts, shredded coconut, and granola are popular choices.
Spoon the chia seed pudding into bowls or jars and enjoy a healthy and delicious treat!
This vanilla chia seed pudding is not only tasty but also packed with nutrients. Feel free to experiment with different flavors by adding cocoa powder, cinnamon, or other extracts

Angel Food Cake with Berries

Ingredients:
For the Angel Food Cake:
1 cup cake flour
1 1/2 cups egg whites (approximately 10-12 large eggs), at room temperature
1 1/2 teaspoons cream of tartar
1/4 teaspoon salt
1 1/2 teaspoons vanilla extract
1 1/2 cups granulated sugar, divided
Zest of one lemon (optional)

For the Berry Topping:
2 cups mixed berries (strawberries, blueberries, raspberries)
2 tablespoons honey or maple syrup

Instructions:
Preheat the oven to 350°F (175°C). Ensure the oven rack is in the lower-middle position.
Sift the cake flour twice and set aside.
In a large, clean, and dry mixing bowl, beat the egg whites with an electric mixer on medium speed until foamy
Add cream of tartar and salt to the egg whites. Continue beating until soft peaks form.
Gradually add 1 cup of granulated sugar, about 2 tablespoons at a time, while continuing to beat the egg whites. Beat until stiff, glossy peaks form.
Gently fold in the sifted cake flour, vanilla extract, and lemon zest (if using) in three additions, being careful not to deflate the egg whites.
Spoon the batter into an ungreased angel food cake pan and smooth the top.
Bake for 35-40 minutes or until the top is golden brown and the cake springs back when lightly touched.
Invert the cake pan over a bottle or cooling rack to cool completely.
In a bowl, gently toss the mixed berries with honey or maple syrup until well coated.
Let the berries sit for about 15 minutes to allow the flavors to meld.
Once the angel food cake is completely cooled, run a knife around the edges of the pan to release the cake.
Place the cake on a serving platter and top with the honeyed berries.
Garnish with fresh mint leaves if desired.
Slice and serve.

Coconut Milk Sorbet

Ingredients:
1 can (14 oz) full-fat coconut milk
1/2 cup granulated sugar or sweetener of choice
1 teaspoon vanilla extract
Pinch of salt
Shredded coconut for garnish (optional)
Fresh mint leaves for garnish (optional)

Instructions:
In a mixing bowl, whisk together the coconut milk, sugar, vanilla extract, and a pinch of salt until the sugar is fully dissolved.
Cover the bowl and refrigerate the mixture for at least 3-4 hours or overnight to ensure it is well-chilled.
Pour the chilled coconut milk mixture into an ice cream maker and churn according to the manufacturer's instructions. This typically takes about 15-20 minutes.
Transfer the churned sorbet to a lidded container and freeze for an additional 3-4 hours, or until the sorbet reaches a firm consistency.
Scoop the coconut milk sorbet into bowls or cones.
Garnish with shredded coconut and fresh mint leaves if desired.
Serve and enjoy this refreshing and dairy-free coconut milk sorbet.
This recipe keeps it simple and uses minimal ingredients. Coconut milk provides a creamy texture without the need for dairy, and the sweetness can be adjusted to your preference.

Papaya and Pineapple Parfait

Ingredients:
1 cup ripe papaya, diced
1 cup fresh pineapple, diced
1 cup Greek yogurt or non-dairy alternative
2 tablespoons honey or maple syrup (optional, for sweetness)
1/2 cup granola (choose a low-acid or homemade version)
Fresh mint leaves for garnish (optional)

Instructions:
Peel, seed, and dice the ripe papaya.
Peel and dice the fresh pineapple
In a bowl, mix the Greek yogurt with honey or maple syrup if you prefer a sweeter yogurt layer.
Adjust the sweetness to your taste.
In serving glasses or bowls, start by layering a spoonful of sweetened yogurt at the bottom.
Add a layer of diced papaya on top of the yogurt.
Follow with another layer of sweetened yogurt.
Add a layer of diced pineapple.
Repeat the layers until you reach the top of the glass or bowl.
Sprinkle a layer of granola on top of the parfait for added crunch.
Garnish with fresh mint leaves for a burst of color and additional freshness.
Serve immediately and enjoy the tropical flavors of this papaya and pineapple parfait.
This dessert is light, fruity, and can be customized to your taste preferences. The combination of papaya and pineapple provides natural sweetness, and the Greek yogurt adds a creamy texture. The granola adds a satisfying crunch to the parfait.

Mango Sorbet

Ingredients:
2 ripe mangoes, peeled and diced
1/4 cup honey or agave nectar
1 tablespoon lime juice
1/2 cup cold water

Instructions:
Blend Ingredients:

In a blender, combine diced mangoes, honey or agave nectar, lime juice, and cold water. Blend until smooth.

Chill Mixture:

Chill the mixture in the refrigerator for at least 1 hour.

Freeze:

Transfer the chilled mixture to an ice cream maker and churn according to the manufacturer's instructions.

Serve:

Scoop the mango sorbet into bowls and enjoy this tropical delight.

Melon Salad with Mint

Ingredients:
2 cups mixed melon balls (watermelon, cantaloupe, honeydew)
Fresh mint leaves, chopped
1 tablespoon lime juice
1 teaspoon honey (optional)

Instructions:
Prepare Melon Balls:

Use a melon baller to create balls from watermelon, cantaloupe, and honeydew.
Mix with Mint and Lime:

In a bowl, combine the melon balls with chopped mint and lime juice.
Drizzle with Honey (Optional):

Optional: Drizzle with honey for added sweetness.
Chill and Serve:

Chill the melon salad before serving for a refreshing and hydrating dessert.

Ginger Infused Pear Compote

Ingredients:
2 ripe pears, peeled and diced
1 tablespoon fresh ginger, grated
1 tablespoon honey
1/2 teaspoon cinnamon
1/4 cup water

Instructions:
Combine Ingredients:

In a saucepan, combine diced pears, grated ginger, honey, cinnamon, and water.
Simmer:

Simmer over low heat until the pears are soft and the mixture thickens to a compote consistency.
Cool and Serve:

Allow the compote to cool before serving. Enjoy it on its own or with a dollop of Greek yogurt.

Cottage Cheese with Pineapple

Ingredients:
1 cup low-fat cottage cheese
1 cup fresh pineapple, diced
Honey or maple syrup (optional, for sweetness)
Chopped mint leaves for garnish (optional)

Instructions:
Prepare the Pineapple:
Peel and dice the fresh pineapple.
Assemble the Dish:
In a bowl, combine the low-fat cottage cheese with the diced pineapple.
Sweeten (Optional):
If you prefer a sweeter flavor, you can drizzle a small amount of honey or maple syrup over the cottage cheese and pineapple mixture. Adjust the sweetness according to your taste.
Garnish (Optional):
Garnish the dish with chopped mint leaves for a fresh and vibrant touch.
Serve:
Serve immediately and enjoy this quick and easy cottage cheese with pineapple snack. This snack is relatively low in fat and acidity, making it a potentially suitable option for those with acid reflux. Cottage cheese provides protein, and pineapple offers natural sweetness. The addition of honey or maple syrup is optional and can be adjusted based on personal preferences.

Baked Sweet Potato Fries

Ingredients:
2 large sweet potatoes, peeled and cut into fries
2 tablespoons olive oil
1 teaspoon paprika
1/2 teaspoon garlic powder
1/2 teaspoon onion powder
1/2 teaspoon cumin
1/2 teaspoon chili powder (adjust to taste)
Salt and black pepper to taste
Optional: Fresh parsley or cilantro for garnish

Instructions:
Preheat the Oven:
Preheat your oven to 425°F (220°C).
Peel the sweet potatoes and cut them into even-sized fries.
Coat with Spices:
In a large bowl, toss the sweet potato fries with olive oil, paprika, garlic powder, onion powder, cumin, chili powder, salt, and black pepper. Ensure that the fries are evenly coated.
Arrange on Baking Sheet:
Arrange the seasoned sweet potato fries in a single layer on a baking sheet lined with parchment paper. Make sure they are not overcrowded to allow for even baking.:
Bake in the preheated oven for 25-30 minutes, flipping the fries halfway through, until they are golden brown and crispy.
Garnish (Optional):
If desired, garnish the baked sweet potato fries with fresh parsley or cilantro for added freshness.
Serve the baked sweet potato fries immediately as a side dish or snack.
This recipe provides a healthier alternative to traditional fried potatoes, and the combination of spices adds a flavorful kick. Sweet potatoes are a good source of fiber and essential nutrients, making them a nutritious choice.
Feel free to adjust the seasoning to your liking, and you can pair the fries with a yogurt-based dip or another sauce of your choice. As always, individual tolerance to specific foods can vary, so be mindful of your body's response.

Yogurt and Berry Popsicles

Ingredients:
1 cup Greek yogurt (or a non-dairy alternative)
1 cup mixed berries (strawberries, blueberries, raspberries)
2 tablespoons honey or maple syrup (adjust to taste)
1 teaspoon vanilla extract (optional)
Popsicle molds

Instructions:
Wash and hull the strawberries, and then cut them into small pieces.
Mix Yogurt and Sweetener:
In a bowl, combine the Greek yogurt with honey or maple syrup. Add vanilla extract if using. Mix well to sweeten the yogurt to your taste.
Layer Yogurt and Berries:
Spoon a layer of sweetened yogurt into each popsicle mold, filling it about one-third of the way.
Add a layer of mixed berries on top of the yogurt.
Repeat the layers until the molds are filled, finishing with a layer of yogurt.
Insert popsicle sticks into the center of each mold, ensuring they are properly centered.
Place the popsicle molds in the freezer and freeze for at least 4-6 hours, or until the popsicles are completely frozen.
Once frozen, run the molds briefly under warm water to loosen the popsicles, then gently remove them from the molds.
Serve these delicious yogurt and berry popsicles immediately and enjoy!
These popsicles are a cool and soothing treat, and the combination of yogurt and berries provides a balance of sweetness and creaminess. The honey or maple syrup adds sweetness without the need for added sugars.

Edamame

Ingredients:
2 cups fresh or frozen edamame in the pod
1-2 teaspoons sea salt (adjust to taste)
Optional: A sprinkle of chili powder, garlic powder, or sesame seeds for added flavor

Instructions:
Prepare Edamame:
If using fresh edamame, rinse them thoroughly under cold water. If using frozen edamame, there's no need to thaw.
Steam Edamame:
Steam the edamame in a steamer basket or microwave-safe dish for about 5-7 minutes, or until they are tender. If microwaving, cover the dish with a microwave-safe cover or damp paper towel.
Season:
While the edamame are still hot, toss them with sea salt. Adjust the salt to your taste preferences.
Optional Additions:
If desired, sprinkle the edamame with chili powder, garlic powder, or sesame seeds for additional flavor.
Serve the steamed edamame immediately, either in the pod or removed from the pod.
To eat, simply pop the edamame beans out of the pod using your teeth or fingers.
Edamame can be enjoyed as a snack, appetizer, or a side dish. They are not only delicious but also a great source of protein and essential nutrients. Additionally, edamame is a versatile ingredient that can be added to salads, stir-fries, or enjoyed on its own with various seasonings.

Cucumber Rolls with Cream Cheese

Ingredients:
1 large cucumber
4 ounces (about 1/2 cup) cream cheese, softened
1 tablespoon fresh dill, chopped
1 tablespoon fresh chives, chopped
Salt and pepper to taste
Optional: Smoked salmon or turkey slices for added flavor

Instructions:
Prepare the Cucumber:
Wash the cucumber and slice it lengthwise into thin strips using a vegetable peeler or a mandoline.
Mix Cream Cheese Filling:
In a bowl, combine the softened cream cheese, chopped fresh dill, chopped chives, salt, and pepper. Mix well until the herbs are evenly distributed.
Spread Cream Cheese Mixture:
Lay the cucumber strips flat and spread a thin layer of the cream cheese mixture over each strip.
Optional: Add Protein (Smoked Salmon or Turkey):
If desired, place a slice of smoked salmon or turkey on top of the cream cheese layer.
Carefully roll up each cucumber strip with the cream cheese and optional protein filling.
Place the cucumber rolls in the refrigerator for at least 30 minutes to allow them to firm up.
Slice and Serve:
Once chilled, slice the cucumber rolls into bite-sized pieces.
Garnish (Optional):
Garnish with additional fresh dill or chives if desired.
Serve these cucumber rolls as a refreshing and flavorful snack.

Sliced Apple with Almond Butter

Ingredients:
1 apple (such as Honeycrisp or Gala), sliced
2 tablespoons almond butter
Optional: a sprinkle of cinnamon or nutmeg for added flavor

Instructions:
Slice the Apple:
Wash the apple thoroughly and slice it into thin rounds or wedges. You can leave the skin on for added fiber.
Spread Almond Butter:
Spread almond butter on each apple slice or wedge.
Optional: Add a Dash of Spice:
If desired, sprinkle a bit of cinnamon or nutmeg on top of the almond butter for added flavor.
Serve:
Arrange the sliced apples with almond butter on a plate or tray.
Enjoy:
Enjoy this simple and nutritious snack!
This snack combines the natural sweetness of apples with the creamy richness of almond butter, creating a satisfying and wholesome treat. Almond butter is a good source of healthy fats and protein, and apples provide fiber and various vitamins.

Hummus and Veggie Sticks

Ingredients:
1 cup homemade or store-bought hummus
Assorted vegetable sticks (carrots, cucumber, bell peppers, celery, cherry tomatoes, etc.)

Instructions:
Prepare the Vegetables:
Wash and cut the vegetables into sticks. You can also include cherry tomatoes or other bite-sized veggies.
Serve with Hummus:
Place the hummus in a bowl or spread it onto a serving plate.
Arrange the Veggie Sticks:
Arrange the vegetable sticks around the bowl or plate with hummus.
Serve:
Serve the veggie sticks with hummus as a delicious and healthy snack.
This snack is not only tasty but also provides a good balance of fiber, vitamins, and minerals. Hummus adds a creamy and flavorful element to the crunchy vegetables, making it a satisfying and wholesome option.
Feel free to customize this snack based on your preferences. You can experiment with different types of hummus (such as roasted red pepper or garlic) or include additional herbs and spices. As always, individual tolerance can vary, so be mindful of your own triggers

Greek Yogurt with Honey

Ingredients:
1 cup Greek yogurt
1-2 tablespoons honey (adjust to taste)
Optional: Fresh berries, nuts, or granola for added texture and flavor

Instructions:
Prepare the Greek Yogurt:
Spoon the Greek yogurt into a bowl.
Drizzle with Honey:
Drizzle honey over the Greek yogurt. Adjust the amount to your preferred level of sweetness.
Optional Toppings:
If desired, add fresh berries, nuts, or granola for added texture and flavor. These can provide additional nutrients and make the dish more visually appealing.
Stir (Optional):
Gently stir the honey into the Greek yogurt to distribute the sweetness evenly.
Serve:
Serve immediately and enjoy your Greek yogurt with honey.
This combination provides a balance of protein from the Greek yogurt and natural sweetness from the honey. It's a versatile dish that you can customize based on your taste preferences and dietary needs.

Mixed Nuts

Ingredients:
1 cup mixed nuts (such as almonds, walnuts, cashews, pistachios, and peanuts)
Optional: A sprinkle of sea salt, cinnamon, or your favorite spice blend

Instructions:
Select Your Nuts:
Choose a variety of nuts based on your preferences. Common choices include almonds, walnuts, cashews, pistachios, and peanuts.
Mix Them Together:
Combine the mixed nuts in a bowl.
Optional Seasoning:
If desired, sprinkle a small amount of sea salt, cinnamon, or your favorite spice blend over the nuts. This step is optional and depends on your taste preferences.
Toss to Coat (Optional):
If you added seasoning, toss the nuts gently to ensure an even coating.
Serve:
Portion out the mixed nuts into small servings, or store them in an airtight container for later use.
Enjoy the mixed nuts as a snack on their own, or pair them with fresh fruit, yogurt, or cheese for added variety.
Remember to be mindful of portion sizes, as nuts are energy-dense. They're a great source of healthy fats, but eating them in moderation is key.

Rice Cakes with Avocado

Ingredients:
Rice cakes (whole grain or plain)
1 ripe avocado
Salt and pepper to taste
Optional toppings: Red pepper flakes, sesame seeds, or a drizzle of olive oil

Instructions:

Prepare the Avocado:

Cut the ripe avocado in half, remove the pit, and scoop the flesh into a bowl.

Mash the Avocado:

Use a fork to mash the avocado until it reaches your desired consistency. You can leave it slightly chunky or make it smoother.

Season the Avocado:

Add salt and pepper to taste. Optionally, you can add a dash of red pepper flakes for some heat.

Spread on Rice Cakes:

Spread the mashed avocado evenly onto the rice cakes.

Optional Toppings:

If desired, sprinkle sesame seeds on top for added crunch or drizzle a bit of olive oil for extra richness.

Serve:

Serve the rice cakes with avocado immediately and enjoy!

This snack is a good source of healthy fats from the avocado and complex carbohydrates from the rice cakes. It's quick to prepare and can be customized with various toppings or seasonings based on your preferences.

Seafood

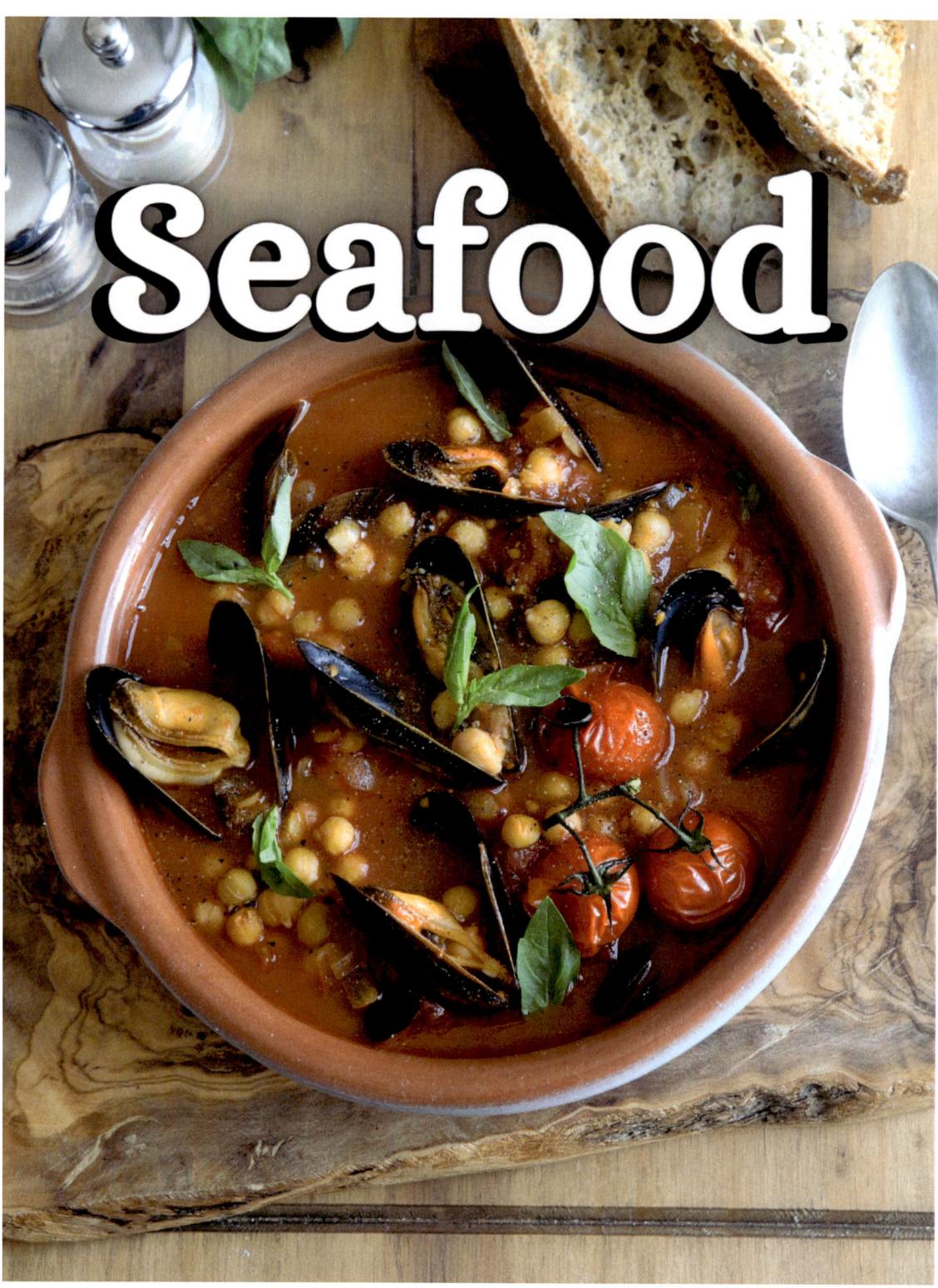

Mussels with Harissa and Basil

Ingredients:

1 pound (450g) fresh mussels, cleaned and debearded
2 tablespoons olive oil
2 cloves garlic, minced
1 tablespoon harissa paste (adjust to taste for spice level)
1/2 cup dry white wine
1/4 cup chopped fresh basil
Salt and pepper to taste
Crusty bread, for serving

Instructions:

Prepare the Mussels:
Scrub and clean the mussels under cold water, removing any dirt and the "beard" (the stringy bit protruding from the shell).
Discard any mussels that are open and do not close when tapped on a hard surface.
Cook the Mussels:
In a large pot or deep skillet with a lid, heat the olive oil over medium heat.
Add the minced garlic and sauté for about 1 minute until fragrant, taking care not to let it brown.
Add Harissa and Wine:
Stir in the harissa paste, coating the garlic with the paste.
Pour in the dry white wine and let it simmer for a minute to slightly reduce and meld the flavors.
Add Mussels and Basil:
Add the cleaned mussels to the pot.
Cover the pot with a lid and let the mussels cook for about 5-7 minutes, shaking the pot occasionally, until the mussels have opened. Discard any mussels that do not open.
Season and Serve:
Once the mussels are cooked and their shells have opened, season with a pinch of salt and a bit of freshly ground black pepper to taste.
Stir in the chopped fresh basil.
Serve:
Divide the mussels and broth between two serving bowls.
Serve the mussels with crusty bread on the side for dipping into the flavorful broth.
Enjoy:
Enjoy the Mussels with Harissa and Basil immediately while they're still hot. Use the bread to soak up the delicious broth.
This Mussels with Harissa and Basil recipe brings together the rich flavors of mussels, the heat of harissa, and the aromatic freshness of basil. It's a wonderful dish for a cozy dinner for two, perfect for enjoying with a glass of wine and good company.

Venetian Shrimp with Polenta

Ingredients:
For the Shrimp:
12 large shrimp, peeled and deveined
2 tablespoons olive oil
2 cloves garlic, minced
1/4 teaspoon red pepper flakes (adjust to taste)
1/4 cup dry white wine
1/2 cup diced tomatoes (canned or fresh)
2 tablespoons chopped fresh parsley
Salt and pepper to taste

For the Polenta:
1/2 cup polenta (cornmeal)
2 cups water
Salt to taste
2 tablespoons butter
1/4 cup grated Parmesan cheese

Instructions:
Prepare the Shrimp:
In a skillet, heat the olive oil over medium heat.
Add the minced garlic and red pepper flakes. Sauté for about 1 minute until fragrant, being careful not to let the garlic burn.
Add the shrimp to the skillet and cook for about 2 minutes on each side until they turn pink and opaque.
Pour in the white wine and let it simmer for a minute to reduce slightly.
Add the diced tomatoes to the skillet and let everything simmer together for another 2-3 minutes.
Season with salt and pepper to taste. Stir in the chopped parsley.

Prepare the Polenta:
In a medium saucepan, bring 2 cups of water to a boil. Add a pinch of salt.
Gradually whisk in the polenta, stirring constantly to prevent lumps from forming.
Reduce the heat to low and continue to cook the polenta, stirring frequently, for about 15-20 minutes until it thickens and becomes creamy.
Stir in the butter and grated Parmesan cheese until well incorporated. Season with additional salt if needed.

Spaghetti with Clams and Garlic

Ingredients:

8 oz (about 225g) spaghetti
1 pound (450g) fresh clams (such as Manila or littleneck), scrubbed and cleaned
4 tablespoons olive oil
3 cloves garlic, thinly sliced
1/4 teaspoon red pepper flakes (adjust to taste)
1/4 cup dry white wine
2 tablespoons chopped fresh parsley
Salt and black pepper to taste

Instructions:
Scrub the clams under cold water to remove any dirt or sand.
Discard any clams that are cracked or do not close when tapped.
In a large pot of salted boiling water, cook the spaghetti according to the package instructions until al dente. Drain and set aside.
Cook the Clams and Sauce:
In a large skillet or pan, heat 2 tablespoons of olive oil over medium heat.
Add the sliced garlic and red pepper flakes. Sauté for about 1 minute until the garlic is fragrant and just starting to turn golden. Be careful not to let it burn.
Increase the heat to medium-high.
Add the cleaned clams to the skillet.
Pour in the white wine and cover the skillet with a lid. Let the clams steam for about 5-7 minutes, or until they open.
Discard any clams that do not open.
Use a slotted spoon to transfer the cooked clams to a bowl, leaving the flavorful liquid in the skillet.
Finish the Dish:
Add the cooked spaghetti to the skillet with the reserved liquid.
Drizzle with the remaining 2 tablespoons of olive oil and toss the spaghetti to coat it in the garlic-infused liquid.
Divide the spaghetti and sauce between two serving plates.
Arrange the steamed clams over the spaghetti.
Garnish and Serve:
Sprinkle chopped fresh parsley over the dish for freshness and color.
Season with salt and black pepper to taste.
Serve the Spaghetti with Clams and Garlic immediately while it's hot.

Grilled Grouper

Ingredients:

2 grouper fillets (about 6-8 oz each)
2 tablespoons olive oil
2 tablespoons lemon juice
2 cloves garlic, minced
1 teaspoon dried oregano
1 teaspoon paprika
Salt and black pepper to taste
Lemon wedges and fresh parsley for garnish

Instructions:
In a bowl, whisk together the olive oil, lemon juice, minced garlic, dried oregano, paprika, salt, and black pepper to create the marinade.
Place the grouper fillets in a shallow dish or a resealable plastic bag.
Pour the marinade over the fillets, ensuring they are well coated. Marinate in the refrigerator for about 30 minutes to 1 hour, turning the fillets halfway through.
Preheat your grill to medium-high heat. Clean and oil the grill grates to prevent sticking.
Remove the fillets from the marinade and let any excess marinade drip off.
Place the fillets on the grill grates. Cook for about 4-5 minutes per side, depending on the thickness of the fillets. The grouper is done when it flakes easily with a fork and is opaque throughout.
You can brush the fillets with any remaining marinade during grilling to enhance the flavor.
Carefully remove the grilled grouper fillets from the grill and transfer them to serving plates.
Garnish the grilled grouper with lemon wedges and fresh parsley.
Serve the grouper fillets with your choice of side dishes, such as rice, grilled vegetables, or a fresh salad.
Grilled grouper is a versatile dish that pairs well with a variety of flavors. The combination of the marinade's citrus and herbs along with the smoky grill marks makes for a wonderful dining experience.
Enjoy your delicious grilled grouper meal!

Fried Oysters with Remoulade

Ingredients:

For the Fried Oysters:
12 fresh oysters, shucked and drained
1/2 cup all-purpose flour
1/2 cup cornmeal
1 teaspoon Old Bay seasoning (or your favorite seafood seasoning)
Salt and black pepper to taste
Vegetable oil, for frying

For the Remoulade Sauce:
1/4 cup mayonnaise
1 tablespoon Dijon mustard
1 tablespoon chopped fresh parsley
1 tablespoon chopped green onion or chives
1 tablespoon capers, chopped
1 teaspoon lemon juice
1 teaspoon Worcestershire sauce
1/2 teaspoon hot sauce (adjust to taste)
Salt and black pepper to taste

Instructions:
In a bowl, whisk together the mayonnaise, Dijon mustard, chopped parsley, chopped green onion, capers, lemon juice, Worcestershire sauce, and hot sauce.
Season the remoulade sauce with salt and black pepper to taste. Adjust the hot sauce to your preferred level of spiciness.
Cover the sauce and refrigerate it until you're ready to serve the fried oysters.
In a heavy-bottomed skillet or deep fryer, heat vegetable oil to 350°F (175°C).
In a shallow dish, mix together the all-purpose flour, cornmeal, Old Bay seasoning, salt, and black pepper.
Dredge each shucked oyster in the flour mixture, shaking off any excess.
Carefully place the coated oysters into the hot oil using tongs. Fry for about 2-3 minutes until they are golden brown and crispy. Be sure not to overcrowd the skillet – fry in batches if needed.
Once the oysters are fried, use a slotted spoon to transfer them to a plate lined with paper towels to drain any excess oil.
Arrange the fried oysters on a serving platter.
Serve the remoulade sauce alongside the fried oysters for dipping.
You can also garnish the dish with additional chopped parsley or lemon wedges.

Tuna Croquettes

Ingredients:

For the Tuna Croquettes:
1 can (6-7 oz) canned tuna, drained and flaked
1/2 cup breadcrumbs
1/4 cup finely chopped onion
1/4 cup finely chopped celery
1/4 cup finely chopped bell pepper (any color)
1/4 cup mayonnaise
1 tablespoon Dijon mustard
1 tablespoon chopped fresh parsley
1 teaspoon lemon juice
1/2 teaspoon garlic powder
Salt and black pepper to taste
1/4 cup all-purpose flour (for coating)
1 egg, beaten (for coating)
Vegetable oil, for frying

For the Lemon-Dill Sauce:

1/4 cup mayonnaise
1 tablespoon lemon juice
1 teaspoon chopped fresh dill
Salt and black pepper to taste

Instructions:

Prepare the Tuna Croquettes:

In a bowl, combine the drained and flaked canned tuna, breadcrumbs, chopped onion, chopped celery, chopped bell pepper, mayonnaise, Dijon mustard, chopped parsley, lemon juice, garlic powder, salt, and black pepper.

Mix the ingredients until well combined. The mixture should hold together when shaped.

Divide the mixture into 4 equal portions and shape each portion into a patty.

Place the flour, beaten egg, and additional breadcrumbs in separate shallow dishes for coating.

Coat each tuna patty first in flour, then dip it in the beaten egg, and finally coat it with breadcrumbs, pressing gently to adhere.

Heat vegetable oil in a skillet over medium heat. Carefully add the coated tuna patties to the skillet.

Cook the croquettes for about 3-4 minutes on each side, or until they are golden brown and heated through.

Once cooked, transfer the croquettes to a plate lined with paper towels to drain any excess oil.

Prepare the Lemon-Dill Sauce:

In a small bowl, whisk together the mayonnaise, lemon juice, chopped dill, salt, and black pepper to create the sauce.

Grilled Lemon Garlic Shrimp

Ingredients:
1 pound large shrimp, peeled and deveined
3 tablespoons olive oil
3 cloves garlic, minced
Zest of 1 lemon
Juice of 1 lemon
1 teaspoon dried oregano
Salt and black pepper to taste
Fresh parsley for garnish

Instructions:
In a bowl, mix together olive oil, minced garlic, lemon zest, lemon juice, dried oregano, salt, and black pepper.
Add the peeled and deveined shrimp to the marinade, ensuring they are well-coated. Allow them to marinate for at least 15-20 minutes.
Preheat the grill or grill pan over medium-high heat.
Thread the marinated shrimp onto skewers.
Grill the shrimp for 2-3 minutes per side or until they are opaque and cooked through.
Garnish with fresh parsley and serve.

Baked Lemon Herb Salmon

Ingredients:
4 salmon fillets
2 tablespoons olive oil
Zest of 1 lemon
Juice of 1 lemon
2 cloves garlic, minced
1 teaspoon dried dill
Salt and black pepper to taste
Lemon slices for garnish

Instructions:
Preheat the oven to 400°F (200°C).
Place the salmon fillets on a baking sheet lined with parchment paper.
In a small bowl, whisk together olive oil, lemon zest, lemon juice, minced garlic, dried dill, salt, and black pepper.
Brush the lemon herb mixture over the salmon fillets.
Bake in the preheated oven for 12-15 minutes or until the salmon is cooked through and flakes easily with a fork.
Garnish with lemon slices and serve.
These seafood recipes focus on using herbs and citrus for flavoring, avoiding ingredients that may trigger acid reflux. Remember that individual tolerance can vary, so it's essential to pay attention to your body's response and make adjustments as needed.

Thank you for choosing to embark on this culinary journey with me and for entrusting me with a small part of your kitchen adventures.

Your support and trust mean the world to me. Every recipe, every technique, and every story shared in this cookbook is a reflection of my passion for food and my desire to bring joy to your tables. Your decision to purchase this cookbook not only encourages me to continue sharing my culinary knowledge but also supports the countless hours of recipe testing, writing, and photography that went into its creation.

Wishing you many happy moments of deliciousness and culinary creativity!

For Zian And Milan, who brings smiles to my face and joy to my heart every day

www.ingramcontent.com/pod-product-compliance
Lightning Source LLC
Chambersburg PA
CBRC090740080526
44730CB00036B/67